better together*

*This book is best read together, grownup and kid.

 akidsco.com

a kids
book
about

a kids book about JUNETEENTH

by Garrison Hayes

A Kids Co.
Editor and Designer Jelani Memory
Creative Director Rick DeLucco
Studio Manager Kenya Feldes
Sales Director Melanie Wilkins
Head of Books Jennifer Goldstein
CEO and Founder Jelani Memory

DK
Editor Emma Roberts
Senior Production Editor Jennifer Murray
Senior Production Controller Louise Minihane
Senior Acquisitions Editor Katy Flint
Acquisitions Project Editor Sara Forster
Managing Art Editor Vicky Short
Publishing Director Mark Searle
DK would like to thank Teara Kuhn

This American Edition, 2024
Published in the United States by DK Publishing
1745 Broadway, 20th Floor, New York, NY 10019

DK, a Division of Penguin Random House LLC

A catalog record for this book is available from the Library of Congress.
ISBN: 978-0-7440-9887-7

DK books are available at special discounts when purchased in bulk for
sales promotions, premiums, fund-raising, or educational use. For details, contact:
DK Publishing Special Markets, 1745 Broadway, 20th Floor, New York, NY 10019, or SpecialSales@dk.com

Printed and bound in China

www.dk.com

akidsco.com

MIX
Paper | Supporting
responsible forestry
FSC™ C018179

This book was made with Forest
Stewardship Council™ certified
paper — one small step in DK's
commitment to a sustainable future.
Learn more at
www.dk.com/uk/information/sustainability

For my Pops, Larry Hayes.

Intro
for grownups

The stories we accept shape how we understand the world around us. There are some stories we've heard a million times—Rosa Parks refusing to give up her seat on the bus, or Dr. Martin Luther King Jr.'s "I Have a Dream" speech. Some stories, however, are hiding in plain sight—tucked away in history books and oral histories, waiting for us to find them, cherish them, and pass them along.

Juneteenth is a story of good news!

For some, the truth of Juneteenth has yet to be discovered; this book is intended to make sure our history isn't hidden again!

My goal in writing it is to bring Juneteenth to life, introducing kids to a powerful account of resilience, joy, and solidarity that will stay with them for a lifetime.

This is a book about

JUNETEENTH.

The word Juneteenth is 2 words combined: "June" and "nineteenth."

Juneteenth celebrates the end of slavery in the United States on June 19, 1865, more than 150 years ago.

You may think slavery ended
when the Civil War was over,
but that's not true.

Hi, my name is Garrison Hayes.

I wrote this book because...

1. The stories of the past help us understand today and build a better tomorrow.

2. I **LOVE** history.

3. My great-great-great-grandparents were enslaved people, here in the United States of America.

In order to understand Juneteenth and my family history, we have to go back, more than...

400 YEARS.

Beginning in the year 1619, African people were brutally captured, sold, forced onto ships, taken far from their homes and families, and brought to what is now the state of Virginia.

And that...

SHAPED AMERICA FOREVER.

America wasn't the first country to embrace chattel* slavery, but it *did* perfect it.

*Any form of slavery is abominable. Chattel slavery is when a human being is considered the property of another person.

Slavery in America was about race: white people enslaved Black people.

It was a cruel, inhumane, and very *profitable* institution.

America became the richest nation in the world because of the free labor of enslaved Black people.

BUT NOT EVERYONE AGREED WITH IT.

Free people who had been enslaved, like Frederick Douglass, spoke about the inhumanity of slavery.

But, because the livelihoods of many white Americans in the South* depended on chattel slavery, by the 1800s they were willing to fight a war over it.

*The states of Texas, Louisiana, Mississippi, Alabama, Georgia, Florida, and South Carolina, and later, Virginia, Arkansas, Tennessee, and North Carolina.

This was called the

CIVIL

The war was fought by the Union army from the North, and the Confederate army from the South.

Some people say it was about each state having the right to choose their own laws.

But it wasn't that simple.

The war was really about slavery.

IN 1863....

while the country was still at war over slavery, President Lincoln made **the Emancipation* Proclamation.**

*To emancipate means to free a person from restraint, control, or the power of another person.

It declared that

"ALL PERSO SLAVES ARE, FORWARD SH

NS HELD AS
AND HENCE -
ALL BE FREE."

The proclamation didn't free everyone, but its message encouraged people to...

KEEP
FIGHTING.

Okay, now let's skip ahead
to the good part...

The Union army finally defeated the Confederate army

Now there was only
one thing left to do...

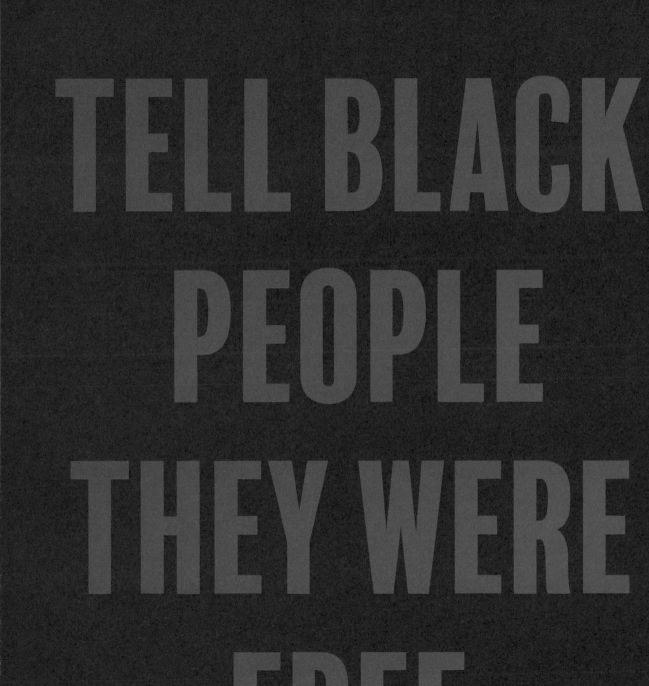

But, back then, there weren't fast ways to get the news out to people—no phones, no TVs, and definitely no internet.

News had to be shared through newspapers or from person to person, by word of mouth.

And on June 19, 1865—around 2 months later—word finally made it to Galveston, Texas, the last place to learn that the war was over and...

As one person found out,

they told another,

and another,

and another.

Black people celebrated their

FREEDOM!

They shouted, they sang, they

REJOICED!

What makes Juneteenth special to me is that even though it isn't the only day Black Americans found out they were free, it was the first day nearly *every* Black American knew they were free.

I wish I could say that's the end of the story and everything was fine every day after.

But I can't.

There were a few good
years after emancipation.

Black people...

traveled freely to find their
families, which had been
separated,

started businesses,

saved millions of dollars,

bought homes,

became senators,

and there was even a
Black governor!

This period of time was
called Reconstruction.

And it was all made possible because Black people in the South were protected by the Union army.

But, that protection didn't last...

IN 1876,

there wasn't a clear winner
of the presidential election.

And to solve it, politicians agreed
to make Rutherford B. Hayes the
president of the United States if
he would remove the Union army
from the South.

It was called the **Compromise of 1877**.

And it completely removed protection for Black people from white people who wanted them under their control.

Much of the success Black people had achieved was erased almost overnight.

We call the time period that started in 1877 Jim Crow.*

*Jim Crow was a demeaning character of a Black man created by a white actor. This name of this made-up character eventually came to stand for racial segregation and outright violence against Black people in America.

AND IT LASTED NEARLY 100 YEARS.

During that time, thousands of Black people were killed and their property was stolen or destroyed.

The joys of Juneteenth celebrations faded away.

You see, Jim Crow laws made it illegal for Black people to do everyday things.

Visiting a public park: **illegal**.

Voting: **illegal**.

In some places, it was even illegal for Black people to laugh in public.

Jim Crow laws were created to keep white people in power and to make racial segregation legal.

Juneteenth became something people celebrated privately and quietly.

Until 1968—over 100 years after the first Juneteenth—when the holiday was brought back into the national spotlight...

At the time of his assassination on April 4, 1968, Dr. Martin Luther King Jr. was working on the Poor People's Campaign. The work Dr. King had begun continued thanks to Coretta Scott King, and Rev. Ralph Abernathy, who connected the movement to Juneteenth.

Nearly 50,000 people joined together at the Lincoln Memorial in Washington, DC, for the movement's Solidarity Day rally.

On June 19, 1968.

This rally brought together people from many backgrounds:

Black and white,

Hispanic and Latino,

Christian,

Jewish,

and Muslim.

All standing in solidarity with one another.

Because Juneteenth is about...

FREEDOM FO

R EVERYONE.

It's the belief that none of us
are free until all of us are free.

And that we can never be
truly free if we forget where
we came from.

Let's skip ahead again.

On June 17, 2021, after a long campaign led by descendants of enslaved people—those like me—Juneteenth was finally declared a national holiday by President Joseph R. Biden.

I believe if there was ever a time we needed a yearly reminder to stand with one another against oppression and for freedom for all,

it's now.

Outro
for grownups

Now that you, and the kid you're reading with know the story of Juneteenth, what comes next? Hold on to the power of its annual reminder that no one of us is free until all of us are free. Consider talking to other kids, friends, and family about ways we can all stand with those still enslaved by systemic racism.

Whether a grownup or a kid, we can ask ourselves questions to set our own personal course of action. Where in our community, country, and world are there people who need us to lift our voices on their behalf? What does solidarity look like in our day-to-day lives? What does allyship mean, and how can we be better allies for marginalized groups? Just as importantly, how can we continue to learn from the stories of the past to better understand our present and build a brighter future?

My hope is that this book is just the beginning of a lifelong love for history and the power of standing in solidarity with those who are still waiting to be set free.